SPOTLIGHT ON
France

Ngeri Nnachi

T0019530

Lerner Publications ◆ Minneapolis

This book is dedicated to everyone who takes pride in learning about the richness of other countries and cultures to inform their own practices.

Read by an expert reader.

Lerner Publications Company
An imprint of Lerner Publishing Group, Inc.
241 First Avenue North
Minneapolis, MN 55401 USA

For reading levels and more information, look up this title at www.lernerbooks.com.

Main body text set in Aptifer Sans LT Pro Semibold.
Typeface provided by Linotype AG.

Illustration on page 13 by Laura K. Westlund.

Designer: Athena Currier

Library of Congress Cataloging-in-Publication Data

Names: Nnachi, Ngeri, author.
Title: Spotlight on France / Ngeri Nnachi.
Description: Minneapolis : Lerner Publications, [2024] | Series: Countries on the world stage | Includes bibliographical references and index. | Audience: Ages 8–12 | Audience: Grades 4–6 | Summary: "France leads Europe's agricultural production and is one of the oldest countries worldwide. Learn more about France's history, economy, government, and more"— Provided by publisher.
Identifiers: LCCN 2022048362 (print) | LCCN 2022048363 (ebook) | ISBN 9781728491974 (library binding) | ISBN 9798765602539 (paperback) | ISBN 9781728496504 (ebook)
Subjects: LCSH: France—Juvenile literature.
Classification: LCC DC17 .N53 2024 (print) | LCC DC17 (ebook) | DDC 944—dc23/ eng/20221018

LC record available at https://lccn.loc.gov/2022048362
LC ebook record available at https://lccn.loc.gov/2022048363

Manufactured in the United States of America
1-53136-51146-2/8/2023

TABLE OF CONTENTS

INTRODUCTION

French Revolution

IT WAS THE SUMMER OF 1789.

French and foreign soldiers filled Paris, the capital of France. Across the country, peasants were fighting for limited resources such as food that had become very expensive and scarce. A revolution was stirring. Common people feared that the French king, Louis XVI, and other privileged people would overthrow their efforts for reform. Looking for weapons and ammunition, a mob stormed the Bastille. This prison in Paris had become a symbol of the harsh rule of the French monarchy. In the countryside, people also decided to take a stand against the wealthy people whose land they worked. They attacked landowners' homes and destroyed work contracts. The French Revolution had begun.

Fighting at the Bastille in 1789

CHAPTER 1

The Creation of a Country

From 500 BCE to 500 CE, a group of Celtic peoples spread from central Europe to Gaul, or what we now know as France. Rome invaded and took over Gaul in the first century BCE. Then in the fifth century CE, a group of people called the Franks conquered the land and gave France its modern name. France comes from the Latin Francia, which means "the country of the Franks." The Franks also brought their language with them. Modern French comes from Latin and has traces of early Frankish too.

French and English soldiers fight during the Battle of Agincourt, part of the Hundred Years' War (1337–1453).

France officially became a country in the ninth century. It is one of the oldest countries in the world. As it became more powerful, it fought many wars to protect and expand its empire. The Hundred Years' War, for example, was a long struggle between England and France over land and about which family had the lawful claim to the French throne. By the end of the Hundred Years' War, France had reclaimed most of its land and was again the strongest European power. Though England continued to try to claim the throne until the nineteenth century, it was never successful.

JOAN OF ARC

Joan of Arc is a national hero in France. After this peasant girl became a military leader in the 1420s, she led France to major victories that helped the country win the Hundred Years' War. The Roman Catholic Church named her a saint in 1920. France has a Joan of Arc Festival every year. Many cities have parades, plays, and other activities in her honor.

The French Revolution took place between 1789 and 1799. King Louis XVI's spending had left the country with little money. People starved because poor harvests and droughts led to a lack of food. Taxes and bread prices were rising. The people of France began to resent the ruling class and the monarchy. They wanted better conditions and rule by the people, not kings and queens. They rose up against the monarchy.

During the French Revolution, people rioted and attacked the royal Tuileries Palace.

A painting of Napoleon Bonaparte in his study

The French monarchy was overthrown in 1792. A republic with a written constitution was born. Not long afterward, in 1804, military dictator Napoleon Bonaparte became the emperor of France. France's First Republic ended. Bonaparte led a series of wars to expand the French Empire across Europe. He was eventually forced to give up his rule of France in 1814 after his disastrous invasion of Russia.

After Napoleon, France had many leaders and different types of rule. France became a global power, conquering and colonizing parts of the Americas, Africa, and Asia. During the twentieth century, France fought in two major wars against Germany: World War I (1914–1918) and World War II (1939–1945). After the defeat of Nazi Germany in 1945, France's Fourth Republic began in 1946. But the government was unstable. Algeria in North Africa, one of France's oldest

In the 1800s, French colonizers took Algiers, the capital city of Algeria.

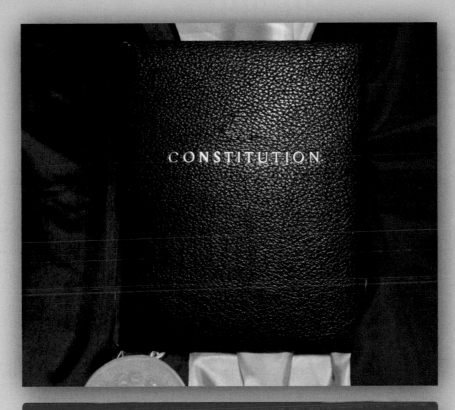

France adopted a new constitution under the Fifth Republic.

colonies, was fighting for independence. The war was controversial in France.

France called on Charles de Gaulle, a famous World War II general, to make France stable again. He helped create a new constitution. France adopted it, and the Fifth Republic began in 1958. Algeria won its independence in 1962. Many other French colonies gained independence around this time. Thirteen overseas territories are still under French control.

CHAPTER 2

Land and Language

France shares borders with many countries. Belgium and Luxembourg are to the northeast. Germany, Switzerland, and Italy lie to the east. The Mediterranean Sea borders France to the south. The Atlantic Ocean forms France's western border.

Around sixty-five million people live in France. About 10 percent of the population are immigrants. The largest group of immigrants come from Algeria. France is also home

to immigrants from other former African colonies, European countries such as Portugal and Italy, and Asian countries such as China.

The Basque people live in southwestern France and northern Spain near the Pyrenees Mountains. These peaks separate France and Spain. The Basque people have a unique culture and language. Other regional languages are also spoken in France, although French is the country's only official language.

About three-fifths of French people are Catholic. France also has one of Europe's largest Muslim populations. Many

In 2019 a Basque Festival took place in Hendaye, France. These festivals celebrate Basque culture, including Basque dance, sports, and food.

French Muslims can pray at the Grand Mosque of Paris, one of the largest mosques in France.

French Muslims come from North African nations such as Algeria and Morocco, which were once French colonies.

Many French people enjoy sports. Soccer, which the French call football, is the most popular sport in France. Almost two million athletes play in French football leagues. The second most popular sport is tennis. The French Open, a Grand Slam event, takes place in France every spring.

CHAPTER 3

France's Diverse Economy

France has a very diverse economy. Its main markets include tourism and manufacturing. The United States and France have a strong trade relationship. The US exports products such as industrial chemicals, computer software, and broadcasting equipment to France. In return, France exports machinery, chemicals, materials such as plastic and leather, and transportation equipment to the US.

France is the most visited country in the world. Over ninety million tourists visit France from all over the world every year. One thing that people like about France is how easy it is to get to and from nearby European countries. Tourists love the food, culture, and beautiful historic buildings there. France also has dramatic landscapes, with rivers, mountains, and beaches to explore. France has some of the world's most famous museums, including the Louvre in Paris.

Tourists may look at art exhibits at the Musée d'Orsay in Paris.

In fact, Paris is a leading global city. It makes up about one-third of France's national wealth. Paris has many popular tourist sites including the Eiffel Tower, Notre Dame Cathedral, the underground catacombs, and the Luxembourg Gardens.

When it comes to fashion, France leads the way. French fashion brands such as Chanel and Louis Vuitton as well as

THE NOTRE DAME CATHEDRAL

In April 2019, a mysterious fire broke out in the Notre Dame Cathedral. The church was being restored, but the fire damaged the inside and outside of it. The fire was probably an accident. One possible cause was a problem with some electrified church bells. Restoration began again in 2020.

Models show off new designs on the runway during Paris Fashion Week.

makeup brands such as Lancôme are famous all over the world. Paris Fashion Week happens twice a year. It is a popular and influential event that includes over one hundred shows by top fashion houses. It draws thousands of journalists and hundreds of photographers. Buyers for stores around the world attend the fashion shows to learn about the latest trends. Many celebrities also attend.

France leads the European Union in agriculture. It produces a lot of wheat, barley, corn, potatoes, and sugar beets. The country also has many vineyards, or fields of grapevines.

CHAPTER 4

A Government for the People

Unlike the United States, France has had several different constitutions. Its most current one was created in 1958 and established the Fifth Republic.

In France, the head of state is the president, and the head of the government is the prime minister. Below the prime minister is a Council of Ministers, also called the cabinet, made up of ministers. The Council of Ministers is the main executive body of the government and was established in the 1958 constitution.

French prime minister Élisabeth Borne speaks at a news conference.

The president is elected every five years by the people of France. Citizens can vote once they are eighteen. The president commands the military. They also name the prime minister and cabinet ministers. The prime minister can introduce bills to the French parliament, the part of the government that makes laws. The parliament has two houses, the National Assembly and the Senate. French voters elect deputies, or leaders of the National Assembly. Locally elected officials choose senators.

An illustration of Napoleon Bonaparte

France has had many notable leaders. One was Napoleon Bonaparte. His efforts to maintain France's power in Europe led to the Napoleonic Wars (1799–1815). Napoleon also reformed the French educational system by making it more available to the middle class and letting states control it instead of churches. He centralized the government and made it more efficient.

THE ROSETTA STONE

In 1798 Napoleon sent a team of about 160 scientists and artists to conduct research in Egypt. An officer in his team discovered a mysterious stone that had three types of writing carved into it: ancient Greek script, ancient Egyptian script, and ancient Egyptian hieroglyphics. It was the Rosetta Stone. In 1801 the British defeated France and seized the Rosetta stone and other relics. They are on display in the British Museum.

France's current president is Emmanuel Macron. He is France's youngest president and was elected in 2017 and again in 2022. During his presidency, Macron has worked on many modern concerns such as tackling climate change and encouraging people to get vaccinated against COVID-19 to help stop the spread of the disease.

Emmanuel Macron gives a speech at the COP27 climate conference in November 2022.

CONCLUSION

Modern France

MODERN FRANCE FACES MANY ISSUES SUCH AS CLIMATE CHANGE. French leaders have pledged to make the country greener. In 2015 France and many other nations met in Paris and adopted the Paris Agreement. The agreement's goal is to reduce carbon emissions and slow climate change. According to their 2019 Energy-Climate Law, France also wants to have net zero carbon emissions by 2050. That would mean the amount of carbon the country gives off would be the same as the amount removed from the atmosphere.

Emmanuel Macron meets other world leaders at the COP26 World Leaders Summit in 2021 to discuss climate change. *Left to right:* Former British prime minister Boris Johnson, Macron, and United Nations secretary-general António Guterres.

France also faces social issues. In 1982 the educational priority zones program started to address education inequality. It funnels extra money to school districts in need, funding resources for students and teachers alike.

Other social problems such as racism, especially against Black people and French Muslims, are on the rise in France. Face coverings were banned in public places in France in 2011. That meant many Muslim people, especially women, could not wear important religious coverings such as the hijab. Lawmakers proposed another law in 2022 to ban face coverings in sports. Not everyone agreed with the ban. Many people protested. And as of 2022, many French citizens continue to work against issues such as racism by speaking up, protesting, and more.

The future of France is bright. French people are making strides to help one another and combat issues such as climate change and racism.

The sun shines on vineyards in eastern France.

TIMELINE

500 BCE–500 CE The Celtic peoples spread from central Europe to Gaul.

843 West Francia, which would later become France, is created.

1180 Philip II, who was also known as Philip Augustus, changes his title from king of the Franks to king of France.

1789 The French Revolution begins.

1790 The National Assembly abolishes the nobility.

1958 France joins the European Union. The Fifth Republic begins, and the current French constitution is adopted.

2015 France commits to a National Low Carbon Strategy for 2050 to tackle climate change.

2019 France adopts the Energy-Climate Law with a goal of net zero carbon emissions by 2050.

2022 Thousands of French citizens gather to protest racism in France.

FRANCE FAST FACTS

Official name: France

Population: 64,677,291

Land area: 210,017 square miles (543,941 sq. km)

Largest city: Paris

Capital city: Paris

Form of government: unitary semi-presidential representative democratic republic

Official language: French

Flag:

GLOSSARY

bill: a draft of a law

colonize: to establish a colony in another place, especially by force

constitution: a document that establishes the basic beliefs and laws of a nation, establishes the powers and duties of the government, and outlines the rights of people living there

controversial: causing disagreement, especially because of opposing ideas or views

dictator: when one person has total rule, control, or leadership of a country

European Union: an economic and political union between twenty-seven European countries, including France

executive: relating to the branch of government that represents a country, oversees laws, and names officials

export: to carry or send something abroad, especially for sale in another country

Grand Slam: one of the four major tournaments in pro tennis, including the Australian Open, the French Open, Wimbledon (in England), and the US Open

monarchy: a system of government where one person, such as a king or queen, has total control

republic: a government that has a head of state who is not a monarch, such as a president

LEARN MORE

Britannica Kids: France
https://kids.britannica.com/kids/article/France/345690

Kiddle: France Facts for Kids
https://kids.kiddle.co/France

Kids World Travel Guide: France Facts
https://www.kids-world-travel-guide.com/france-facts.html

Kissock, Heather. *Paris*. New York: AV2, 2022.

Layton, Christine. *Travel to France*. Minneapolis: Lerner Publications, 2024.

Loh-Hagan, Virginia. *The French Revolution*. Ann Arbor, MI: Cherry Lake, 2021.

National Geographic Kids: France
https://kids.nationalgeographic.com/geography/countries/article/france

Walker, Tracy Sue. *Spotlight on the United States*. Minneapolis: Lerner Publications, 2024.

INDEX

PHOTO ACKNOWLEDGMENTS

Image credits: Artwork by Anonymous, courtesy of Wikimedia Commons, p. 5; Artist unknown, courtesy of Wikimedia Commons, p. 7; North Wind Picture Archives/Alamy Stock Photo, p. 8; Everett Collection/Shutterstock, p. 9; agefotostock/Alamy Stock Photo, p. 10; pitchal frederic/Getty Images, p. 11; Dayow/Shutterstock, p. 14; zijin/Shutterstock, p. 15; Luboslav Tiles/Shutterstock, p. 17; Pete Douglass/Getty Images, p. 18; FashionStock.com/Shutterstock, p. 19; Horacio Villalobos#Corbis/Corbis/Getty Images, p. 21; mikroman6/Getty Images, p. 22; LUDOVIC MARIN/AFP/Getty Images, p. 23; Anadolu Agency/Getty Images, p. 25; © Marco Bottigelli/Getty Images, p. 27.

Cover: Image Source/Getty Images.